ATOMIC

Education

Animal
SPIES

PAUL MASON

Raintree

www.raintreepublishers.co.uk
Visit our website to find out more information about Raintree books.

To order:
☎ Phone 44 (0) 1865 888112
▤ Send a fax to 44 (0) 1865 314091
▢ Visit the Raintree bookshop at **www.raintreepublishers.co.uk** to browse
  our catalogue and order online.

First published in Great Britain by
Raintree, Halley Court, Jordan Hill,
Oxford OX2 8EJ, part of Harcourt
Education. Raintree is a registered
trademark of Harcourt Education Ltd.

© Harcourt Education Ltd 2008
First published in paperback in 2008.
The moral right of the proprietor has been asserted.

Editorial: Melanie Waldron and Harriet Milles
Design: Victoria Bevan, Steve Mead,
  and Bigtop
Illustrations: Darren Lingard
Picture Research: Mica Brancic
Production: Julie Carter

Originated by Modern Age
Printed and bound in China by Leo Paper Group

ISBN 978 1 4062 0685 2 (hardback)
12 11 10 09 08
10 9 8 7 6 5 4 3 2 1

ISBN 978 1 4062 0706 4 (paperback)
12 11 10 09 08
10 9 8 7 6 5 4 3 2 1

**British Library
Cataloguing in Publication Data**
Mason, Paul, 1967–
Animal spies. – (Atomic)
591.5
A full catalogue record for this book is available from
the British Library.

Acknowledgements
The publishers would like to thank the following for
permission to reproduce photographs:
ardea.com pp. **9**, **17** (M. Watson), **10** (Auscape/Nicholas
Birks), **13** top (Thomas Dressler), **21** top (Adrian Warren),
26 (A.L. Stanzani); Corbis/L. Clarke p. **6** top; FLPA pp. **5**
top & bottom, **14** top, **18**, **25**, **27** (Minden Pictures), **21**
bottom (R. Dirscherl), **22** (Dembinsky Photo Ass.); Getty
Images pp. **13** bottom (National Geographic), **29** (Taxi);
NHPA pp. **11** (Alan Williams), **6** bottom (Stephen Dalton);
Photolibrary/Picture Press p. **14** bottom.

Cover photograph of an owl reproduced with permission
of OSF/Mark Hamblin. Photograph of a bear reproduced
with permission of NHPA/Andy Rouse.

Every effort has been made to contact copyright holders
of any material reproduced in this book. Any omissions
will be rectified in subsequent printings if notice is given
to the publishers.

The publishers would like to thank Nancy Harris, Dee Reid,
and Diana Bentley for their assistance in the preparation
of this book.

Disclaimer
All the Internet addresses (URLs) given in this book were
valid at the time of going to press. However, due to the
dynamic nature of the Internet, some addresses may
have changed, or sites may have changed or ceased to
exist since publication. While the author and publishers
regret any inconvenience this may cause readers, no
responsibility for any such changes can be accepted by
either the author or the publishers.

It is recommended that adults supervise children on the
Internet.

Contents

Some words are printed in bold, **like this**. You can find out what they mean in the glossary. You can also look in the box at the bottom of the page where the word first appears.

SPIES ALL AROUND!

What do we mean by "animal spies"? Animal spies are similar to their human counterparts. Like James Bond or Alex Rider, their special skills or senses give them an advantage over the competition.

Why become a spy?

Why do some animals need to acquire special spy skills or senses? There are several reasons:

✳ To enable them to track down their prey.

✳ To help them locate safe places to eat or drink.

✳ To avoid being caught by **predators**.

✳ So they can defend themselves against surprise attacks.

predator   **animal that hunts other animals for food**

Find out what this mother bear is doing on page 16.

Find out how this shark sniffs out its prey on page 18.

Who's that spying out a victim? See page 8.

Find out about a mole's nighttime spy skills on page 22.

Spy Techniques

How do the animal kingdom's spies hunt down their victims, or defend themselves from attack? They have a wide variety of techniques.

Animal methods

✴ SNIFFING THINGS OUT
Some animals have a powerful sense of smell, which enables them to sniff out **predators** or prey.

✴ CAREFUL LISTENING
Sensitive hearing is invaluable. With good hearing, even the quietest noise can be heard – whoever is making it!

✴ PATIENCE
Some animals patiently lie in wait for prey; others keep very still, waiting for a predator to leave before they move again.

✴ TEAMWORK
Smaller animals work as a team to set up **sentries**, in case danger threatens.

sentry   lookout

CRAFTY CROCODILES!

There are predators out there who skillfully, secretly spy on their victims. They invisibly sneak up on them, attacking at the very last moment.

Underwater walker

When a crocodile spies an animal coming to the riverbank for a drink, it stealthily sinks to the bottom of the river. Slowly, it creeps along the riverbed towards its victim.

The drinker does not spot the crocodile, but the "croc" can see the drinker! At the last moment the crocodile launches itself out of the water like a rocket. It bites its victim and pulls the animal down into the water, never to be seen again.

The saltwater crocodile is the most dangerous kind. It can be very aggressive, and every year people are attacked by "salties" as they are called.

That's amazing!

Crocodiles have strong muscles for closing their jaws - but weak ones for opening them.

This crocodile's prey could be the photographer, unless he gets out of the way – fast!

This peregrine falcon is "still hunting", which means it is spying out prey before taking off to hunt it.

PEREGRINE FALCON

HABITAT: worldwide

FAR-SIGHTED FALCONS

Imagine how valuable seeing long distances would be to an animal spy. One such spy can see things as clearly as a pair of binoculars with 10 times magnification!

The spy in the sky

Peregrine falcons have amazing eyesight, which they use while flying to spy on birds far below them.

When the peregrine spots its prey, it drops from the sky like a stone. Its tremendous speed – around 300 kph (186 mph) – makes it the fastest animal on Earth! The peregrine rams into its victim, catches it in mid-air, and then flutters slowly down to Earth.

That's amazing!

When a peregrine swoops down, a third eyelid closes to keep its eyes from being damaged.

WATCHFUL MEERKATS

Not all animals use their eyesight for hunting. Some use their eyes to locate predators that might be hunting them!

MEERKATS HABITAT: dry areas in southern Africa

Defensive team

Meerkats have developed a sophisticated defensive system. A few meerkats act as **sentries**, and keep watch for predators. The remaining meerkats continue with their daily lives.

Different dangers

If the sentries see a hawk overhead they let out a distinctive squeak. Then all the meerkats hide in the burrows where they are safe from airborne attack. However, if the lookouts spot a snake they have a different squeak. Then the meerkats leave the burrows so that the snake cannot trap them inside.

Meerkat sentries watch from the highest piece of ground. Even up here, they stand on their hind legs for a better view.

The sentries have spotted a hawk – everyone rushes underground!

The owl's forward-facing eyes help it to zero in on its prey.

Owls are skilled at silent flying. They glide down and grab their victims without warning.

OWLISH SPIES

One animal spy has such excellent night vision, people assume it must be able to see in the dark.

OWLS
HABITAT:
worldwide

Nighttime hunter

Owls mostly hunt at night, because they can see amazingly well in almost no light. There are several reasons for this:

* Large eyes – a snowy owl's eyes weigh the same as a human's!

* Oblong-shaped eyes let through more light than human eyes.

* Forward-facing, wide-apart eyes mean the owl is good at judging distances in the dark.

* Eyes packed with light-sensing devices called rods – five times as many as a human's.

That's amazing!

The tawny owl has the best night vision of all: it sees in the dark about 100 times better than a human!

BEAR ALERT!

Animals use a variety of senses to spy out predators or prey. Many use their sense of smell.

BEAR
HABITAT: polar regions and temperate forests around the world

Sniffing out a meal

Bears have an unusually strong sense of smell which they constantly rely on. Some experts believe that smell is as useful to bears as sight is to humans.

Bears follow a "path" of scent that is blown on the wind. One black bear in California went 4.8 kilometres (3 miles), in a straight line, to the body of a dead deer. It stopped to sniff a few times, just to make sure it was still travelling in the right direction.

That's amazing!

Polar bears have been known to follow the smell of a dead seal more than 16 kilometres (10 miles)!

This polar bear has sniffed something good! Some bears are drawn to food from many kilometres away – if it smells delicious enough!

SNIFFY SHARKS

Animals also use their sense of smell for hunting in water habitats. Some animals can follow a smell through water to its source, in the hope that there will be a meal at the end.

Killer trackers

Among the deadliest ocean trackers are sharks such as the great white shark. As it swims along, water flows over two spots, like nostrils, which it uses to sniff out tiny amounts of blood in the water.

SHARKS
HABITAT:
oceans
worldwide

Sharks can "smell" a drop of blood in 94 litres (25 gallons) of water. That's less than one drop in a bath of water!

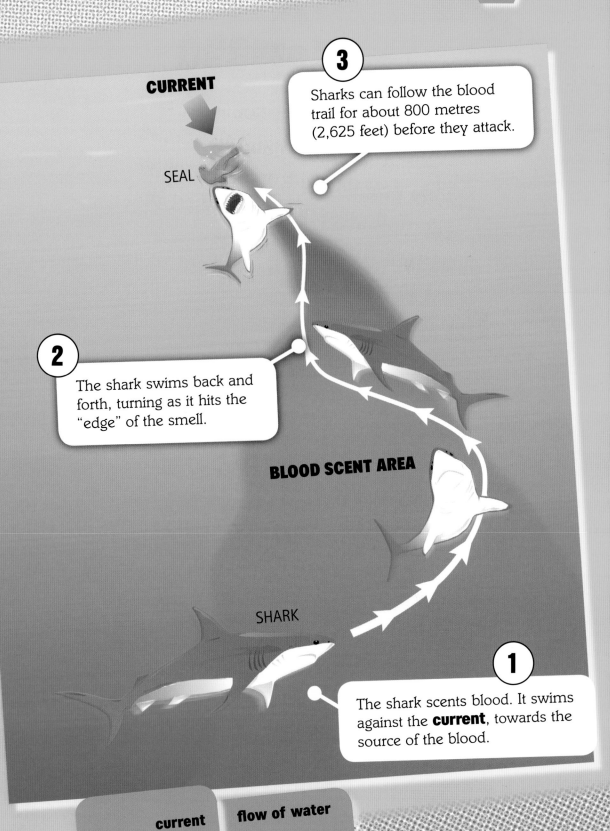

CURRENT

3 Sharks can follow the blood trail for about 800 metres (2,625 feet) before they attack.

SEAL

2 The shark swims back and forth, turning as it hits the "edge" of the smell.

BLOOD SCENT AREA

SHARK

1 The shark scents blood. It swims against the **current**, towards the source of the blood.

current   flow of water

CRAFTY KOMODO DRAGONS

Komodo dragons are giant lizards that closely resemble dinosaurs. The dragons use scent to track down food from far away.

KOMODO DRAGON
HABITAT: Lesser Sunda Islands, Indonesia

A nasty bite

Every dragon's mouth is full of **infectious** bacteria. Even a small bite is lethal enough to kill the dragon's prey over a period of days. The dragon nips its victim and then tracks it. The victim takes days to die, during which time the dragon waits until its prey is too weak to resist. Then it finally moves in and starts to eat – sometimes while the victim is still alive!

Fast food!

Komodo dragons are fast eaters! A 46-kg (101-lb) dragon once ate a 41-kg (90-lb) pig in 20 minutes. That's like a 45-kg (100-lb) person eating 320 quarter-pound hamburgers!

infectious   likely to spread disease

A Komodo dragon can smell a meal from 8.5 kilometres (5 miles) away!

The dragon's huge jaws mean it can eat massive mouthfuls!

As the mole burrows through the earth, it uses its nose to spy out earthworms, its favourite food.

There are 22 fleshy "fingers" on the star-nosed mole's nose.

The shortest pair of "fingers" are the most sensitive.

NOSEY MOLES

Imagine living in a world of complete darkness, where you had to **navigate** your way around using your sense of touch. It would take a **unique** spy to succeed in a place like that!

Nosey feeler

The star-nosed mole spends the majority of its time underground. Amazingly, it feels its way around not with its paws, but with its nose!

Over 100,000 nerves run from the mole's nose to its brain. That's more than six times as many as go from your hand to your brain.

STAR-NOSED MOLE
||||||||||||||||||||||||||||||||
HABITAT: marsh and wetland, eastern North America

navigate   find the way

unique   one of a kind

SQUEAKY BATS

Imagine what it would be like to be able to fly through a blanket of darkness without crashing. What a skillful nighttime spy you'd be!

BATS
HABITAT:
worldwide

Night flyer

Bats are the finest nocturnal flyers in nature. Their diet includes fast-moving flying insects that come out in the evening. Bats can easily catch the insects, but how do they spot them in the first place?

Bats use a system called **echolocation**.

As bats fly along, they send out a squeak.

If the squeak hits an insect, it bounces, or echoes, off and back to the bat.

As soon as the bat hears a returning squeak, it changes course and heads for the insect. A few more squeaks and the bat catches its prey!

This round-eared bat has caught a meal that looks about twice the size of its own head!

echolocation · using sound that bounces back to you as a way of finding something

A dolphin's smooth skin hides some amazing spying tools!

Clicks go out

Clicks bounce back

DOLPHIN CLICKERS

A few animals have an extra bit of equipment that helps them spy on targets they cannot see!

Underwater trackers

Dolphins use an intricate system of clicking noises to stalk prey they cannot even see. First they send out a "click" from a special chamber in their head. The click travels through the water; when it hits something, it bounces back to the dolphin like an echo.

The returning click tells the dolphin what is out there. It immediately sends out another click. If this one bounces back more quickly than the first, the dolphin knows it is getting closer to its prey.

That's amazing!

Dolphins can use their click system to find objects even when they are blindfolded!

Dolphins use their eyes during the last moments of a hunt.

ON THE SCENT!

Some animal spies have outstanding eyesight, or a keen sense of smell, while others have amazing skills like echolocation. But which animal is the best at tracking down its targets?

Top tracker

One of the most talented animal trackers is the bloodhound. Bloodhounds have been specially bred to follow a trail of smell for amazing distances. Experts say that bloodhounds will follow a trail for more than 161 kilometres (100 miles).

Criminal catcher

For many years, bloodhounds have been used to track down escaped criminals. The most famous bloodhound tracker was called "Nick Carter". Nick is said to have tracked over 600 criminals in the state of Kentucky in the United States!

receptor | sender of smell signals to the brain

A bloodhound's nose contains 40 times as many smell **receptors** as a human's.

Slits at side of the dog's nose flare out to allow more smell to flow in.

Long ears drag along the ground, stirring up smell.

Glossary

current flow of water. Rivers have a current that flows towards the sea. The sea also has currents, as water moves from one area to another.

echolocation using sound that bounces back to you as a way of finding something

infectious likely to spread illness. A cold is infectious, for example, because it can be spread from one person to another.

navigate find the way. Humans do not have the natural skills of some animals so we generally have to use maps to find our way.

predator animal that hunts other animals for food

receptor sender of smell signals to the brain. The more receptors an animal has, the better it will be able to smell.

sentry lookout watching for intruders. Sentries normally watch from places where they will have a good view or a good chance of stopping an intruder.

unique one of a kind

Want to Know More?

Books

* *Amazing Creatures* series, John Townsend (Raintree, 2004)

* *Amazing Nature: Night Movers*, Matt Turner (Heinemann Library, 2004)

* *Animals Under Threat: Great White Shark*, Richard and Louise Spilsbury (Heinemann Library, 2005)

* *Animals Under Threat: Peregrine Falcon*, Mike Unwin (Heinemann Library, 2004)

Websites

* www.flmnh.ufl.edu/fish/Sharks/ISAF/ISAF.htm
  This scary website is full of information about shark attacks.

* www.komodo-gateway.org/
  The website of the Komodo National Park, where most of the world's Komodo dragons live.

If you liked this Atomic book, why don't you try these...?

Index

Notes for adults
Use the following questions to guide children towards identifying features of report text:
Can you find an example of a general opening classification on page 4?
Can you give an example of a generic participant on page 7?
Can you find examples of the details of an owl's night vision on page 15?
Can you find examples of non-chronological language on page 23?
Can you give examples of present tense language on page 27?